KETO DIET FOR BEGINNER #2021

The essential Guide for men and women to a Ketogenic Lifestyle

By

Anna Lor

TABLE OF CONTENTS

INTRODUCTION 3
CHAPTER ONE: HEALTHY DIET? 4
    What is a Healthy Diet Meal Plan? 4
    Things to Think About When Meal Planning 6
    Meal Plan Diet - Why It's For You 9
    Diets - Handling Failure 11
    Rating the Fad Diets 14
CHAPTER TWO: KETO DIET FOR BEGINNER 21
    What is Keto? 21
    The Ketogenic Diet 22
    Keto Diet Benefits 23
    How To Formulate A Keto Diet? 25
    Keto Diet for Beginner 31
    Keto Dieting? Here Are 10 Foods You Must Have in Your Kitchen 32
    Net Carbs 33
    Low-Carb and Keto Diet Fast Food Menu Choices: How to Eat Successfully at Restaurants .. 35
CHAPTER THREE: KETOGENIC DIET PLAN 40
    Tips for You to Start 40
CONCLUSION 42

INTRODUCTION

Many people have mixed feelings about whether the Ketogenic diet is good for you or not; as a Ketogenic diet person, I will tell you why I think the Keto diet is very great for your health. It's probably not for everyone now, but if it's something you thought about lately, let me help you make your mind easier.

The ketogenic diet is a very powerful weight loss program. It uses high fat and very low carbohydrates to burn fat rather than glucose. Many people know the Atkins diet, but the keto plan limits even more carbohydrates. When we are surrounded by fast foods and refined foods, avoiding carbohydrates can be a task; however, preparation can assist. Here are a couple of products of a keto diet.

As so many people now hop into the "ketogenic diet" vehicle, more and more people are beginning to question if this diet is for them. Even if you're not on a ketogenic diet, you'd be hard-pressed to see those foods now in your store. Sellers are conscious that the ketogenic diet does not seem to go exactly where they wanted it and start to make pleasant snacks "ready to go." Can you please?

CHAPTER ONE: HEALTHY DIET?

What is a Healthy Diet Meal Plan?

Knowing what foods to eat is vital to reduce the risk of gout as well as to treat gout, a kind of arthritis that is caused by an abnormally high level of uric acid in the blood. Urika is a material that develops as your body breaks down the matter called purines, the natural substance which is found in the body. all cells of your body and the food that you consume.

One of the good and delicious foods to eat with gouty arthritis is dark fruit. What are these? What are these? Try cherries and blackberries and blueberries and violet grapes. The latest studies have shown that cherries have been associated with lower uric acid levels. In different meals, you can replace those ingredients with cherries. You can make cherry pancakes, for example, instead of making banana pancakes. Consult your doctor to see which particular fruits can supplement your gout diet, who will also know the diets that are best for you.

In normal situations, people assume that health is a living being without sickness, and it is also hard to explain what health really is, but health can certainly be preserved utilizing good habits and a balanced diet. The implementation of safe eating behaviors is the secret to good health. We have attempted to establish below, through suggestions and tips, what a balanced diet food plan is so that you can handle it according to your needs and desires.

1. The first step in a balanced diet plan is to split your meal into five or six smaller meals each day, with each meal eaten maximum for one or two days.

2. Including nutritious and tasty food snacks if you feel hungry.

3. Plan your food for one week, and a range of foods and ingredients must be available. You have to prepare your snacks in advance.

4. Stop fast food, candy, ice cream, cookies, and chocolates.

5. Crackers, dried and fresh fruit, popcorn, milk, pretzels, low-fat cheese, baby carrots, popcorn air, peanut butter, and nuts and seeds can be a part of your diet.

6. Drink more water in a day and particularly before eating. It holds your body fluid properly and also makes you less hungry.

7. Reduce the use of fats and discourage the use of a lot of milk, margarine or butter, chicken, mayonnaise, and use less oil in the intended cooking.

8. Soft drinks and juices have higher vitamins to keep them from being used.

9. Add more grains to your diet, as whole grain bread can be used instead of white bread and brown rice.

10. Do not use high-frequency sugar foods and consume vegetables at every meal.

11. Never miss breakfast as your metabolism rises, and appetite decreases later on.

12. Feed very slowly and don't feed much else. As the food is often unregulated while studying or watching TV.

13. Collect the number of the recipe so that these can be used in the preparation of a dietary meal plan.

14. When you prepare for basic foods, it allows you to have a wide variety of foods, and you repeatedly eat almost every wholesome item.

15. You can also prepare a packed lunch in the form of good sandwiches. It keeps you away from junk or fast food and even lists sandwiches to alter the taste periodically.

16. Try not to replicate the same meal on the same day and instead use multiple foods for all foods.

17. Keep nutritious food packed in your cabinets and refrigerator. Easy, fast food ingredients and standbys will help you keep your diet plan safe.

18. There should be a balanced diet meal schedule in a week, two vegetarian meals, two fish meals, one poultry meal, and one red meal.

19. Buy a wide variety of fruits and vegetables and eat in a meal many vegetables.

20. Plan meals that also have safe cooking methods. No more fried food. No more fried foods.

21. You may also enjoy other favorite foods, which have a higher amount of calories, but very less and rarely.

22. An exercise regimen, along with your diet plan, can also be performed to burn extra calories.

23. Investigate what kind of vitamins, minerals, and calories a food form contains, and then use the diet meat plan that you or your family have drawn up for yourself.

Things to Think About When Meal Planning

The diet has three main components: carbohydrates (essential for the body's energy generation), protein (essential for controlling and sustaining the functions of the body and a large portion of the macro mass of the body), fat (cellular structure, immune system function, and hormonal production). Many foods have these in combination. When we eat new, nutrient-rich foods and balance our diet with nutritious carbohydrates, proteins, and fats, our body meets and retains its weight and overall health. You should try to find the good balance you need to fuel your body with the following types of foods. The frequency, quantity, and time of day, these types of foods are essential to your energy, appearance, and overall health. Below we describe the groups that you can carry every day with your meal plan and what they do for your body.

Sources of protein- (vegetarian, non-vegetarian)
- Milk sources
- Food and vegetables.
- Fruit
- Fats
- Starches Once Daily
- Starches

Why does the body use protein?

Protein is essential for a body because it helps our cells to expand and heal. It is the protein amino acids that form the building block of each cell. So, when you think about how the human body is a complex cellular organism composed of trillions of cells that are dying and need to be replaced daily, protein is important in our diets! Did you know that you have a fresh digestive tract every 28 days or so? That's right! That's right! The cells in our digestive system fully replace each other every 28 days.

Protein is also nice because it allows blood sugar to be controlled. Amino acids are also used in the body to build up lean muscle mass. Protein's molecular structure is very complex. It also needs more energy to metabolize protein for the body. Only put: You burn more calories as protein-rich foods! It's nice to improve your source of protein by selecting various kinds of food and finding a variety of proteins based on plants and animals.

* * Not all proteins are produced on a par with each other. Protein has nuts, whole grains, and veggies. They do not, however, contain all 9 of the essential amino acids that your body requires to build lean muscle.

* * * Vegetarians have to be a little more imaginative to ensure that the required amino acids that the body needs are stored. One common mistake is that incomplete proteins that do not contain all the essential amino acids are not consumed. One way to meet this challenge is to combine incomplete proteins with complimentary food. An example would be peanut butter with whole wheat bread or brown rice beans. Vegetarian sources such as hemp seed, tofu, sweet wheat, and quinoa contain full proteins (which contain all essential amino acids).

Dairy of milk:

For several purposes, Dairy is integrated into a balanced middle strategy. Dairy can be a calcium source, an added protein source during the day, ideal as a condiment or for important probiotics (found in yogurt), which are important to digestive health. A balanced digestive system contributes to loss of weight.

* * Cheese is a dairy that can also be used in a vegetarian diet as a source of protein. However, it can be very caloric, and more than a portion of the food can be consumed very easily. Catch 1 oz can be a perfect way to include cheese in a meal plan. Cheese serving over a starch or vegetable.

Fat is a weight loss buddy and wellbeing overall:
Fats are required in the body to help both transport and absorb fat-soluble vitamins. For our common health and for the protection of our internal organs, fats are essential.

* * Avocados and nuts are great to soothe body inflammation. Saturated and unsaturated fats are required. Transfats need to be avoided.

Vegetables are the best friend to lose weight and maintain a healthy weight.
Find variation in your choice of vegetables. Mix them together and prepare them so that you can enjoy them. Find harmony between raw and cooked foods, as they are a great source of healthy carbohydrates, fiber, and little protein. Most significantly, vegetables provide the body with essential macronutrients that many people suffer deficiencies. New vegetables also help to minimize body inflammation.

* Key for vegetarians: Be sure to put the vegetarian type of "Veg."
* * Hypothyroidism individuals should avoid eating cruciferous vegetables as raw. Cruciferous vegetables comprise: cauliflower, broccoli, springs of brussels, asparagus, chocolate, cucumbers, bell peppers, garlic, turmeric, mustard greens, greens, and turf. Soy products are also considered to cause hypothyroidism problems for people.

Once Daily Starch:

Any whole grain falls into the group of the Once Regular Starch. Foods in this group are strong energy foods that provide the body with a positive nutrient balance and are important for the production of energy. It is essential to look at the serving sizes while attempting to lose weight. Stars are important to the body. Without these starches, blood glucose and insulin levels are vulnerable to excess in the body.

* Think of them as sluggish carbohydrates. If you reach plateaus with weight loss, try including them in your breakfast meal to encourage the body to burn the carbohydrates all day long.

Starches:
All carbohydrates are divided into sugar. The absorption of sugar is slowed down by the fiber in these starches. Your body needs to work properly with carbohydrates. Quality is important.

Fruit:
The fruit is wonderful! Fruits are wonderful! They deliver natural sweetness and are rich in fiber. They also supply significant macronutrients and antioxidants to the body. Fruits are essential to cellular damage repair. In order to prevent future fruit weight increases, only portion sizes should be known.

Herbs:
Herbs perform best when they are fresh and natural. They help to minimize inflammation in the body and can improve food's taste.

It's all about controlling the food intake and preserving it. You don't have to be a perfectionist or an extremist. You just have to drive for balance.

Meal Plan Diet - Why It's For You

A food plan diet is a safe choice for weight loss over the long term. Hundreds of diet plans are to be selected. Some of them have undergone the time test, and others are just on the horizon. If you, like most people, you go from the plan to the right one for you. The plan itself will decide whether or not you are losing weight. Regardless of what it promises, you won't lose weight if it's badly put together. Run the other way if you see a diet plan that promises quickly and easily to lose weight. Loss of weight is hard work; discipline and dedication are required. It's even harder than it was to lose weight. The most successful food plan helps you to lose weight and keep it away.

A diet for a meal plan has many benefits:

Help you get healthy eating. When preparing meals, you choose meals from each of the food groups needed to make every meal. Your body performs better when you eat healthily and knows how to burn fat more effectively. You burn more calories as your metabolism rises.

You give versatility. Give flexibility. You can vary the food you eat while you remain within the meal plan diet. Foods that may be considered cheating on other diet plans, you should eat, and it just becomes a part of the meal by incorporating other of these 'wants.' You can't eat any pizza, but you can make the diet a lot easier to stick with by moderating some of your favorite foods.

Portion control aid. Portion control aid. We know how various calories we want to consume for the day, many times, but we are struggling to get the right nutrient blend. How many fats, carbohydrates, or fiber calories do we need?

Savings time and money. You will save money in the grocery shop by not ordering food in advance by preparing your meals. You make and stick to your list. You also can not eat fast food while preparing your meals, even though you want something from the balanced menu.

Most meal plan diets recommend eating many small meals all day long. This keeps the body's metabolism up and more effectively burning calories. Five meals of approximately 300 calories each provide most people with the calories required to stay healthy and feel full and very few to lose weight.

Diets - Handling Failure

Life is the process of trial and error where failure and success are two sides of the same coin.

What's different with nutrition?
Dieting is the same in some respects and different in some respects from most other items.
It's still the same because success and failure would go together-two sides of the same coin.
It's different because, let's face it, in the first place, you don't even want to diet. And you probably have negative dietary thoughts and emotions.
Everybody wants to stroll, read, drive a car, have a great career and a great companion. Nobody needs a diet.

The connotations of "dieting" are negative.
And then if you struggle or fall off your diet, you prefer to blow this insufficiency out of proportion, finding an excuse – conscious or unconscious – to leave, since you start the diet first and foremost with negative thoughts and feelings.
And when you interrupt your diet, you eventually think of yourself as a failure, come down and blast your ego, self-confidence, and self-esteem.

After some time, the pain of the loss is gone.
That's when you're able to try out the next trendy diet. The latest figures show that dieticians "test" 4 new diets a year on average.

Here lies the real big difference in diet. That's the issue.
You don't learn to improve diet from past mistakes. You will tackle your next diet just as you did your last failed diet. And the one left of that and the one left.

Certainly, you're changing diets. You move from low-fat to high-protein to low-carbon to stable and continuing cardiac.

But you don't change the way you eat.

It's a wonderful phenomenon. You learned how to walk by falling down a lot of times, and you learned something every time you fell, and the next time you walked, you were a little smarter.

Just as much as you fall at diet and get up and try another thing, the next time, you do not get any better. Or next. Or next.

While every failure in life gives our minds and bodies useful input to learn to improve and give us more tough mental abilities for the next attempt, it doesn't seem to work for diet.

Why failure is not working in dieting

There are many reasons why diet failure doesn't help you learn to eat the next time.

You never give up walking, reading, driving, etc. You will never "remain" these things willingly and, therefore, would have allowed yourself the chance to be a "failure" of them. You have never blower your pride, your self-esteem, and your self-assurance. It was never a choice for you to fix them, failure, or leave, so you had to learn from your mistakes.

You see the other events in life as the ends. Dieting is never an end ... it's the road to the end ... so it's totally different. You should give up "this" diet, knowing that someone else will still be around the corner. You finish ... well ... whatever it is for you: to look and feel sleek and sexy; to get the job you have been hungry for; to regain your pride and confidence; to wear a bathing suit or swim trunks without a shock; to play with your kids without getting stuck; to impress your friend at your high school meeting; healthy for a long time .... Furthermore, you should (and do) still blame the diet if you avoid or struggle to diet. "Oh, that diet isn't working or didn't work for me." But if you keep failing the driver test, you can't blame your vehicle.

You have never learned how to diet properly-using all the natural strengths that you have can successfully help you diet. You were encouraged and taught walking and reading and all the other things that we mentioned. But nobody has ever taught you your personal Dieting Compatibility Stylet, so you end up doing a tough job (dieting) without the expertise, help, and information required for it.

Set it all together
Failure's a professor. It's nothing but an instructor.

In most life fields, you can use any failure as a learning step to achieve your objectives. Failure is teaching you and making you tough.

But because dieting never constitutes your aim or your end game-it's just the way to end-you're never profoundly inspired to eat.

You probably confuse dieting with your real target-this sexy body, for instance-but you know it isn't at any stage.

It's easier to give up your diet than most items in your life, but when you avoid taking a new diet, you always feel the pain of failure without the useful learning experience.

You've got another diet failure when you're already looking forward to your sexy body and not better prepared for the next diet than the last one.

Regardless of a diet you choose, there are scientifically-based food methods that use your natural strengths and approach your diet to emphasize those strengths and bend your approach to your diet to use those strengths to your benefit.

The first step is when to figure out what the particular diet style(TM) is and how you can use it.

Though you think diet should be intuitive and all the advertisements make you believe that this time it will be easy, your experience and experiences of some 75 million U.S citizen adults on a diet right now and who will struggle to eat it repeatedly shows that it is neither easy nor intuitive.

Dieting successfully is an ability that you have to master and practice to succeed. It's not a hard skill to master. But it is almost difficult to succeed in dieting without diet-as most of us have proved over and over again.

Performance and failure are the same coins on two sides.

It's time to place diets in the right light, learn from mistakes in the past, and use the experience to make the next diet the last diet.

You can just as easily walk or drive your car if you do it correctly.

Rating the Fad Diets

How do we understand what works and what is healthy for so many different diets? The best way to make sure you discover the history of the author and the study behind the nutritional approach. Any good diet should provide a history and experience of the author in the fields of nutrition and biochemistry. But even a broad summary does not mean a healthy and credible diet. However, at least it indicates that the author has some dietary information. The research behind the diet shows that the diet is not something that was developed by the scientist, given that the research does not serve itself and adjust to a hypothesis.

Some diets do not need a lot of tests and studies simply because they are focused on basics. For example, many feminine magazines have nutritional write up and weight loss, but it is a good sense that most weight issues should already know that 'eat smaller foods,' 'diminish sugar and fat,' etc. are traditional ideologies. More organized diets should offer some scientific explanations for their suggested effectiveness, preferably case studies, and regular test testing, as well as athletes.

Since we have decided that a balanced diet should be used to choose healthy foods and that RDA minima should be collected, the diets can now be calculated according to those basic parameters. Start with a score of

200 and deduct 10 points for each statement below where the diet is granted. An optimal diet should be 200, but a score of 160 or higher is appropriate.

1. The diet which does not contain sufficient quantities of food classes. Some faded diets exclude one or more of the food groups. Do not subtract 10 points when the nutrients of a food group (e.g., calories, proteins, fats, fibers, vitamins, and minerals) are properly replaced by those of food group in another.
2. The diet doesn't provide at least 45% of its calories from sources of carbohydrate. At least 150 g of glucose/day is needed to prevent ketosis. That's 33-50% of the overall consumption of calories in 1200 calories. Take into account that's the minimum. For extremely active people, this number can increase to 60% at times, i.e., right after exercise.
3. The quality of carbohydrate is more than 20% concentrated sugar. At least 80 percent of the source of carbohydrate must be complex in fruits, seeds, and legumes, ideally.
4. The protein content is more than 30%. A high intake of protein is unhealthy, puts extra pressure on the urinary system, and is a low energy source. Also, for growing children and adolescents, 30% is more than sufficient. Only those who have recently undergone significant injuries (e.g., leg amputation), illness, or surgery need higher intakes of proteins. These people are, however, treated for by a doctor with a special high protein diet.
5. Protein content constitutes 15% or less of total calories. While in large quantities excessive, protein has many important functions, including tissue repair and enzyme production.
6. Fats surpass 30% of the overall consumption. In addition to raising this risk of cardiovascular disease, high-fiber diets have not been shown to reduce weight better than other 'right' eating practices.
7. The net intake of fat is less than 15 % of the total calories. Fat in moderate quantities is important for a balanced diet, which gives

many foods a taste. For most people, fat intakes below 15 percent for long periods are impractical. Fat intake that is too low can hurt children and adolescents who need plenty of calories to develop continuously.
8. Total intake of fat is less than 25 percent essential fatty acids, and more than 30 % of the total intake of fat is saturated fat. For each of them, ten deducts.
9. The diet does not signify traditional foods, which means that foods can be purchased from any food shop or market.
10. Dietary foods are costly or monotonous. Many of the diets require that the purchase of the foods or pricey 'organic' foods only from health food stores. Some foods taste so bad that they are hard to handle again and again (e.g., seaweed). For each of them, ten deducts.
11. The diet consists of a meal schedule that is inflexible. The diet does not allow substitution or variation, which allows a person to live 'home arrested' every day with the same food range.
12. There are fewer than 1200 calories a day in the diet. More than that and the basic functions of your body may not get the energy, vitamins, and minerals you need to work properly, and your dietitian will almost always feel hungry. Diets below 1200 kcalories for those under the care of a dietitian or licensed physician should be reserved.
13. The food needs to be supplemented. If the diet is energy-saving and well-balanced, supplements are not necessary. 'Fat accelerators,' such as the ephedrine, can increase weight loss rates, but the diet should be able to sustain itself. Some food clinics endorse a wide variety of fat accelerators and herbal preparations, and these clinics are making money-not as nutritionists in their expertise or ability.
14. The diet does not prescribe a practical weight target. Diets are not meant to endorse the body of a Greek god or supermodel. You should not recommend that a person loses 100 pounds (even if

overweight is 100 pounds). Diets do not advocate weight loss below optimum weight.
15. The diet advises or encourages weight loss of more than 1-2 lbs/week. You should Do not expect to lose more than 1-2 pounds of fat a week-unless it is chronically obese; at this time, it might be possible to lose 3 pounds. If more than two pounds are lost every week, a loss of water and/or muscle tissue induces the body's change. Gimmicks promising 10 pounds in 2 weeks are either not real, or anything but fat is lost. Bear in mind also that the more weight a person needs to lose and the less a person has, the harder and slower it will be to lose additional weight.
16. The diet does not provide a dietary habits measurement. Diet should be a gradual process in which a person changes usual eating behaviors. It does not include the search for fast solutions and strategies that offer short cuts or drastic changes – one person will never stick with these programs, and those diets do not operate long-term. The number of calories consumed, the food range, and their quantity should be regularly reevaluated ... Maybe once every 1-2 months to assess the success of the programme.
17. Regular exercise, as part of the weight-loss strategy, is not recommended. Weight loss happens twice as quickly with exercise, and there is a more serious risk of losing lean muscle tissue and fat without exercise. That's not fine.

VARIOUS DIETS OVERVIEW

Low carbohydrate diets: there is ketosis, and this has the same problems as fasting. After glycogen is expended (which happens rapidly with athletes and regularly), glucose should be generated from protein sources, and thus it is more wearable on the kidneys. Even with a high diet of proteins, some protein is taken from body tissue to provide enough nervous system energy and daily exercise. The initiation of ketosis is a sign that this phase has started and is not a good feature irrespective of what fatty authorities say.

Great loss of weight in a low carb diet is noticeable because carbohydrates retain water to a ratio of 1:3 in muscles.

As carbon intake decreases, water retention also decreases. Much water flushes to retain water molecules due to a lack of glycogen. In addition, excess nitrogen flushes with even more water by growing protein intake as the kids use water to dilute the nitrogen concentration.

After quitting a low-carb diet and loading up muscles with glycogen, fluid levels increase, and the dietary supplement regains some weight.

Low-calorie diets consisting mainly of protein have the same problems as fasting and low carbohydrates diets of 400-600 kcalories: proteins are used to minimize energy, while the weight is mostly extracted from water. Low-calorie diets should be carefully monitored by a doctor and used as a last resort for those who are not evidently able to lose weight with other approaches. But even those people appear to recover much of their weight when they switch to a healthy diet.

Beverly Hills Diet-a a diet made up of grapefruit, eggs, rice, and celp; minerals and vitamins are insufficient.

Cambridge diet-a high calorie (300-600 kcal per day); a combination of protein and carbohydrates with mineral imbalances; dieter is near fasting.

"Fake" Mayo diet -this diet is made up of grapefruits, eggs, rice, and kelp; mineral and vitamin deficiency.

F-Plan Diet – is high fiber (30-35g / day) calorically diluted diet; it is low in fat and animal products; the absorption of minerals is poor because of fiber.

LA Costa Spa Diet – this diet encourages weight loss of 1-1 lbs/day and is split between 800, 1000, and 1200kcal / day, and is composed of twenty-five percent protein, 30% fat (essentially polyunsaturated), and 45% carbohydrate.

Medifast Diet-this diet is nutritionally healthy but only offers 900 kcal per day, which makes the use of liquid formula monotone, which costly.

Nutriment Diet / Medifast Diet-this is a nutritionally balanced diet; it contains only 900 kcal/day, rendering it monotonous and costly by using liquid formulas.

Optifast diet: this diet is nutritionally healthy, but provides 900 kcal a day. It is monotonous and costly with liquid formulas.

Pritikin Permanent Weight-Loss Diet — it's a nutritionally unbalanced diet; certain days have calorific limitations; diet shifts portions of carbohydrate, protein, and fat; the diet is produced from high protein (100 g / day); vitamin B12 is poor unless properly selected foods.

Prudent diet-a a healthy diet of 2400kcal / day for men; low in cholesterol and saturated fats; fat deriving from a maximum of 20-35% of calories, with emphasis on protein, carbohydrates, and salt; sufficient intake in fish and shellfish and polyunsaturated fats are supplemented with saturated fat.

The quick diet weighs loss-this diet is nutritionally unbalanced; caloric limits some days; the dieter changes sections of carbohydrate, protein, and fat, while low carbohydrates (20-50 g / day) and high fat and protein; meat (saturated fat and cholesterol) eaten with this diet is high.

The diet begins at 500 kcal/day, consisting of two meals a day with one fruit, one potato, one slice of bread, and two exchange of meat; the second week restricts the amount of carbohydrates with the majority of foods coming from the meat community and eggs and cheese and some vegetables; the week 3 includes fruit; the week 4 raises the number of vegetables; week 5 introduces the amount of fat cooked by the dieter;

Slendernov Diet – this diet is nutritionally unbalanced; certain days are low in calories; the dietary diet changes the portions of carbohydrates, protein, and fat; the protein, in general, is large (100 g / day); unless the food is properly picked, vitamin B12 may be deficient.

Weight monitor diet – this diet is nutritionally balanced with approximately 1000-1200 kcal; high-nutrient diet is consumed; inexpensive and palatable food is one of the most popular diets with no real health risks.

A diet of wine-roughly 1200 kcal/day, 28 menus, and a slice of dry table wine for dinner; in addition to the therapeutic components of wine, people are believed to minimize the portion of their diet when eaten from wine; cholesterol- and saturated fats-low; fish, poultry, and veal with moderate quantities of red meat are the main components of this diet.

Yogurt Diet — this is the main dairy dish eaten in breakfast or lunches or snacks, with its diet of 900 to 1000 kcal/day and 1200 to 1500 kcal/day; it is high in protein and low in cholesterol, saturated fat, and refined carbohydrates.

CHAPTER TWO: KETO DIET FOR BEGINNER

What is Keto?

The body normally uses glucose as the main energy source of food. When you eat very few carbs and moderate quantities of protein (excess protein can be converted to carbohydrates), your body transfers its fuel supply to fat. The liver produces fatty ketones (a fatty acid type). These ketones are fuel for the body, particularly the brain that absorbs a great deal of energy and can be used on glucose or ketones.

When the body releases ketones, a metabolic syndrome called ketosis occurs. The best way in achieving ketosis is to fast. If you quickly or consume just very small quantities of carbs and protein, the body transforms into burning stored fat for heat. That's why the diet appears to lose more weight.

Keto's diet requires long stretches at a very low level (not more than 30 g per day) or almost zero g per day of carbohydrates and growing your fats to a high level (to the degree that they will make up up as little as 65 percent of your total intake of macronutrients). In this state of ketosis, the body should be more likely to use fat for energy- and research says that. As you deplete your carbohydrate and glycogen liver and then switch to the fat for food, you must finally be shredded.

From Monday to Sat 12 pm (afternoon) (or Sat 7 pm, depending on the version of which you read, you follow the specific platform. Then your big car up from this moment to 12 o'clock on Sunday night (up to 36 hours later) ...

(Some suggest that, and that is also determined by your body, you can take nuts into the carbohydrate and consume whatever you like, and then there are others who, from my point of view, only stick to clean carbohydrates even throughout your carb.)

The Ketogenic Diet

The ketogenic diet is an ideal choice for many people for weight loss. It's really different and encourages a dietary person to consume a diet that contains food you can't predict.

Therefore, the ketogenic diet or keto is a diet made up of very low carbohydrates and high fat. How many meals are there where you can start your day with bacon and eggs, plenty of them, then follow them for lunch with the chicken wings, and then steak and broccoli for breakfast. This might sound too good for many to be valid. Yeah, this diet is a fantastic day to eat, and with the meal plan, you followed the rules exactly.

If you eat a very limited quantity of carbohydrates, the body gets ketosis. What this means is that the body burns energy fat. How little is the quantity of carbs to eat to get into ketosis? Well, it varies between individuals, but it is good to remain below 25 net carbs. Many would recommend that you remain under ten net carbs while you are in the "induction" period while you actually bring your body into ketosis.

Let me help you when you are not that sure what net carbs are. Net carbs are the quantity of carbs that you consume less dietary fiber. If you eat 35 grams of net carbohydrate and 13 g of dietary fiber per day, your net carbohydrate will be 22 for the day. Simple enough, right?

And what else is good about keto besides weight loss? Many people speak about their increased mental clarity while they are on their diet. Another advantage is an improvement in energy. Another, though, is a diminished appetite.

One thing to think about when taking the ketogenic diet is what is called "keto flu." This isn't encountered by everyone, but it can be hard to do so. You can feel lethargic and have a headache. It's not going to last long. If you feel like this, make sure you have plenty of water and rest.

If it sounds like a diet you'd like to be interested in, what are you waiting for? Dive heard in keto first. You cannot believe the findings in such a short time.

Keto Diet Benefits

Keto is not a fresh diet. It began in the 1920s as a medical procedure to treat epilepsy in infants, but until recently, when anti-epileptic medications came out on the market, the diet became blind. Given its success in reducing the number of seizures in epileptic patients, there is growing research on the dietary potential for treating various neurological conditions and other forms of chronic diseases.

- **Neurodegenerative diseases**. A new study shows the advantages of keto in Parkinson's, Alzheimer's, autism, and MS. It can also defend against injuries and strokes in the brain. One explanation for the neuroprotective effects of keto is that ketones released during ketosis give brain cells additional fuel that can help these cells resist inflammation damage caused by these conditions.
- **Obesity and weight loss**. If you want to lose weight, the Keto diet will help you access your body fat and release it. Constant malnutrition is the greatest challenge when you try to lose weight. The keto diet helps prevent this because reducing carbon consumption and increasing the intake of fat promotes satiety, which makes adherence to diet easier for people. In a study, obese participants lost twice the amount of weight in a low-carb (20.7 lbs) diet in 24 weeks compared with a low-fat diet (10.5 lbs).
- **Type 2 Diabetes**. Besides losing weight, the keto diet also increases the sensitivity of insulin, which is good for those with type 2 diabetes. Research published in Nutrition & Metabolism shows that diabetics with low-carb keto diets have been able to dramatically reduce their reliance on diabetes and even potentially reverse it. In addition, other health factors, including triglyceride reduction and LDL (bad) cholesterol, and an increase in HDL (good) cholesterol, are increased.

- **Cancer**. Most people do not know that the key fuel for cancer cells is glucose. This means that eating the right diet will help avoid the development of cancer. Since the keto diet is very low in carbohydrates, sugar is the main source of fuel for cancer cells. When the organism creates ketones, healthy cells will use that as energy, but not as cancer cells, to destroy them hunger. Studies on keto diets have also shown decreased tumor growth and increased survival for many cancers as far back as 1987.

The major difference between the keto diet and the traditional American or Paleo diets is that it contains far less carbohydrates and far more fat. The keto diet contributes to ketosis, with ketones circulating between 0.5-5.0 mM. This is possible with a home blood ketone detector with ketone test strips. (Please be aware that urine test ketones are not accurate.)

7-Keto Benefits a Weight Loss Regimen

In a number of processes in the body, 7-Keto-DHEA is a naturally occurring active metabolite of the hormone DHEA. 7-Keto-DHEA levels decrease over existence, but levels with supplementation can be restored to normal. Users get classical 7-keto benefits, including lower cortisol, better immune efficiency, and easier weight loss and retention.

How 7-Keto-DHEA to Work

7-Keto-DHEA mainly increases the rate of weight loss by increasing the thermogenesis temperature of the body. Other supplements such as DHEA, caffeine, and ephedrine improve thermogenesis, but these drugs also have undesirable side effects, such as high blood pressure. Improving thermogenesis is one of the most significant 7-Keto advantages without any side effects. In addition, 7-Keto can also be used in very large doses without causing toxicity. One research found that no harm was done to test animals by consuming a 40.000 mg equivalent a day, about 200-400 times the normal 100 or 200 mg daily prescribed dose.

The increased metabolic rate of 7-Keto-DHEA helps dieters to continue to benefit after their diets have begun. Instead of suffering from slow metabolism caused by a low-calorie diet, consumers experience steady metabolism and prevent plateau losses.

The thyroid hormone T3 is boosted by 7-Keto as well. Some supplements for weight loss, such as l-tyrosine, increase fat intake by can T3, but T3 levels inevitably crash when used. On the other hand, 7-Keto retains high T3 levels in users allowing pounds to be continuously shed. Scientists have noted that this increase in T3 stays within a healthy, natural range, allowing users to reap the benefits of increased T3 while preventing too much downfall.

7 Keto weight control Advantages

7-Keto-DHEA itself is not a magical weight loss supplement that helps users lose their fat easily. In conjunction with diet and preparation, however, the main 7 Keto benefits of cortisol reduction, increased T3, and increased thermogenesis make weight loss much easier. 7 Benefits from Keto include reducing cortisol, encouraging people to practice more, and more during their regimes. This is just one way to promote weight loss with 7-Keto-DHEA.

In addition to its other benefits, 7-Keto-DHEA increases the body's use of insulin and prevents fat gain. Compared to other modern weight loss supplements, 7-Keto covers more facets to make nutritional efforts a severe edge.

How To Formulate A Keto Diet?

1. Carbohydrates

To achieve ketosis (getting ketones in above 0.5 mM), most individuals need carbohydrates to be restricted to between 20 and 50 grams (g)/day. The exact amount of carbs varies between individuals. In general, the more resistant an organism is to insulin, the more resistant it is to ketosis. Some insulin-sensitive exercise athletes can eat more than

50g / day and stay ketosised, whereas people with type 2 diabetes and insulin resistance may need to be nearer to 20-30 g / day.

For the measurement of carbs, the use of net carbs is permitted, that is to say, total carbs less fiber and sugar alcohols. Net carbon is only meant to contain carbon dioxide that raises blood sugar and insulin. The fiber has no metabolic or hormonal effect, and most sugar alcoholics have no such effect. The exception is maltitol that can influence blood sugar and insulin without insignificant consequences. Therefore, sugar alcohol should not be excluded from total carbs if maltitol is included in the list of ingredients.

The amount of carbon which could be absorbed and maintained in ketosis can also change over time based on keto modification, weight loss, workout habits, drugs, etc. You should then calculate the ketone levels on a regular basis.

Overall, diets are not adapted to carbohydrate foods, such as pasta, cereals, potatoes, rice, beans, candy, sodas, juice, and beer.

Most milk products contain lactose (milk sugar) carbs. Some, however, have fewer carbs and can be used daily. These include hard (parmesan, cheddar), mild, high-fat (brie) cheeses, full-fat milk cheeses, high-fat milk, and sour cream.

In general, a carb amount of less than 50 g / day breaks down to:
- 5-10 g of protein-based food carbs. Eggs, cheese, and coquillages hold a few remaining grams of carbs and added marinades and spices from natural sources.
- 10-15 g of non-starch vegetables.
- 5-10 g of nut/seed carbohydrates. Most nuts have 5-6 g of carbs per ounce.
- 5-10 g of fruit carbs including strawberries, olives, tomatoes, and avocados.
- 5-10 g of carbon from different sources such as low-carb sweets, high-fat dressings, or very small quantities of sugary beverages.

Beverages

Most people need at least half a gallon a day of the total fluid. Organic coffee, Filtered water, and tea (unsweetened, regular and decaf) and non-sweetened amond and cocoon milk are the best sources. Dietary sodas and beverages are best avoided, as artificial sweeteners are present. When you drink white wine or red wine, you should limit your dryer to 1-2 glasses. If you drink spirits, avoid mixed drinks that are sweetened.

2. Protein

A keto diet is not a diet that includes high proteins. This is because protein increases insulin and can be transformed into glucose through a mechanism known as gluconeogenesis, and also prevents ketosis. However, the protein intake must not be too poor, as it can lead to muscle tissue loss and function.

The average adult is around 0.8-1.5 g of lean body weight per kilogram (kg) a day. The measurement based on lean body mass, not total body weight, is significant. The explanation is that fat mass requires no protein, only the lean muscle mass.

The requirement for protein may range from 44 (= 54.55 x 0.8) up to 82 (= 54.55 x 1.5) g / d if an person weighs 150 lbs (or 150/2.2 = 68.18 kg) and has a body fat content of 20 percent (or a lean body mass of 80 percent = 68,18 kg x 0.8 = 54.55 kg.), for example.

People immune to insulin or taking the keto diet for medicinal purposes (cancer, epilepsy, etc.) should try to get closer to the lower protein boundary. For those really healthy or athletic, the higher limit is. For someone else who uses a keto diet to lose weight or other health benefits, the daily protein amount should be anywhere between them.

High-quality protein sources include:
- Grass-fed meats (6-9 g protein/oz)
- Organic eggs (6-8 g of protein/egg)

- Animal sources of omega-3 fats, such as salmon, sardines, and anchovies, and herrings, captured in Alaska wild. (Protein / oz 6-9 g)
- Seeds and Nuts, such as almonds, macadamia, flax, pecans, sesame seeds, and hemp, (4-8 g protein/4 cup)
- Vegetables (1-2 g protein / oz)

3. Fat

The majority of the diet comes from fat, having determined the exact amount of carbohydrates and protein to eat. A keto diet must be high in fat. When enough fat is consumed, the weight of the body is preserved. If weight loss is needed, less dietary fat should be ingested, and instead, body fat retained for energy expenditure.

The daily fat intake for individuals who eat 2000 calories a day is approximately 156-178 g / day. Fat intakes can also reach 300 g / day for large and highly active people with high energy demands who maintain weight.

Most people may handle high-fat consumption, but some conditions, such as removal of the gallbladder, can influence the amount of fat that can be eaten at a single meal. More regular food or use of bile salts or lipase-high pancreatic enzymes can be helpful.

Stop eating unhealthy fats such as trans fat, heavily processed, polyunsaturated vegetable oils, and high quantities of polyunsaturated omega-6 fats.

The best foods for obtaining high-quality fats are:
- Coconuts and coconut oil
- Avocados and avocado oil
- Grass-fed butter, beef fat, and ghee
- pastured heavy, Organic cream
- Olive oil
- Medium-chain triglycerides (MCTs)

- Lard from pastured pigs

MCT is a particular fat type that is metabolized differently than normal fatty acids in the long-chain. Well before glucose, the liver may use MCTs to generate energy quickly, enabling increased production of ketones.

As for supplements, concentrated sources of MCT oil are available. Many people use them for ketosis. Coconut oil is the only food that is special in MCTs. About two-thirds of the cocoa fat comes from MCT.

Who Should A Keto Diet Be Cautious?

A keto diet is really healthy for most people. However, some people need to take extra precautions and speak to their physicians before they start such a diet.

- Those who take diabetes drugs. Dosage can need to be changed as the diet of low-carb blood sugar decreases.
- People who take high blood pressure drugs. The dosage will need to be changed as a low-carbon diet lowers blood pressure.
- Breastfeeding individuals do not take the strictest low-carb diet because the body will lose around 30 g of carbs a day via milk.

Thus, during breastfeeding, get at least 50 g of carbs per day.

- Kidney disease patients should consult their physicians before eating a keto.

Common Concerns of A Keto Diet

- **Could not achieve ketosis.** Make sure that you don't consume too much protein and that there are no secret carbs in the foods you eat.
- Consume fat forms such as highly processed polyunsaturated maize and soybean oils.
- **"keto-influ" symptoms**, such as feelings of lightheadedness, dizziness, headaches, tiredness, brain fog, and constipation. The

body appears to excrete more sodium when it is ketosis. If you don't get enough sodium from your diet, keto-flu symptoms can develop. This can be remedied simply by drinking 2 cups of broth (with added salt) a day. If you exercise vigorously or have a high sweat rate, you can need to add more sodium again.

- **Dawn effect**. Standard blood fasting sugars are less than 100 mg/dl, and most ketosis patients exceed this level unless they are diabetic. However, blood sugars tend to rise in some people, particularly in the morning, when using a keto diet. This is known as the "dawn effect" because of the natural circadian increase of morning cortisol (stress hormone), which causes the liver to produce more glucose. If this occurs, ensure that you do not eat extra protein at dinner and that you do not sleep too near. Stress and inadequate sleep can also contribute to elevated levels of cortisol. You might also require more time to reach ketosis if you are insulin resistant.
- **Low athletic results**. It normally takes about four weeks for keto-adaptation. During which we turn to something less intense rather than hard exercises or preparation. After the adjustment phase, sports performance typically goes back to normal or better, particularly for endurance events.
- **Keto-rash** is not a typical dietary side-effect. Probable causes include acetone production in sweat, including protein or minerals, which irritates the skin and nutrient deficiencies. Shower right after exercise and make sure that all foods are thick and nutrient-dense.

- **Ketoacidosis.** This is a very unusual occurrence when blood ketone levels are greater than 15 mm. Ketoacidosis is not caused by a well-formulated keto diet. Such conditions, such as type 1 diabetes for SGLT-2 inhibitors or breastfeeding, need more caution. Symptoms include vomiting, nausea, lethargy, and shortness of breath. The sodium bicarbonate mixed with apple juice or diluted orange can solve mild cases. Significant symptoms require urgent medical treatment.

Is Keto Safe For Long Duration?
This is a contentious area. While no studies have demonstrated any harmful long-term effects that can influence a keto diet, many experts now agree that the body will develop "resistance" to ketosis if it does not consistently go in and out of it. Furthermore, a long-term diet of very high fat may not be appropriate for all types of species.

Diet of Cyclical keto
When you are able to reliably produce more than 0.5 mM of ketones in the blood, it is time to get the carbs back into the diet. Instead of only eating 20-50 g carbs/day, on those Carb Food Days, you may want to raise it to 100-150 g. Usually, it would be enough 2-3 times a week. Ideally, it is often achieved on training days during which you increase your protein intake.

This cycling method will make the diet more appealing to some people who are hesitant to replace some of their favorite foods permanently. It may also lower the resolve and dedication of vulnerable individuals to the keto diet or cause binges.

Keto Diet for Beginner

It now seems as if everyone is talking about the ketogenic diet-the low carbon hydrate, moderate protein, a high-fat diet plan that turns the body into the fat-burning machine. The Hollywood stars and athletes have been promoting the benefits of this diet openly, from dropping weight, preventing inflammation, decreasing blood sugar, reducing the risk of cancer, increasing energy, and slowing aging. But is keto something you should consider? This will clarify what this diet really is about, the benefits and drawbacks, and the issues.

Keto Dieting? Here Are 10 Foods You Must Have in Your Kitchen

The ketogenic diet is a popular program for weight loss. It uses high fat and low carbohydrates to burn fat instead of glucose. Many people know the diet of Atkins, but the keto method eliminates carbs even more.

Since we are surrounded by fast-food restaurants and processed foods, avoiding high carbon foods can be a challenge, but careful preparation can help.

The Plan menus and snacks at least a week in advance, so you are not just wrapped up in high-quality meals. Study online keto recipes; there are some nice recipes to choose from. Taking yourself into the keto diet, find, and stick with your favorite recipes.

Some products are staples of a keto diet. Make sure that these things are available:

1. Eggs-Used as omelets, hard-boiled as an eggplant, quiches, low carbohydrate pizza crust, and more.

2. Bacon-Is there a justification I need? Breakfast, salad, burger topper, blackberry (no toast, of course; try a BLT in a cup, thrown into mayo)

3. Cream cheese-hundreds of dishes, crusts of pizzas, main dishes, desserts

4. Shredded cheese Sprinkle with taco meat in a bowl made from microwave tortilla chips, salad tops, low-carb pizza, and shrimp.

5. Lots of Romaine and Spinach-Fill the green veggies; be prepared for a fast salad when hunger strikes

6. EZ-Sweetz liquid sweetener — The use a few drops instead of sugar, which is the natural and easiest to use an artificial sweetener I found

7. Cauliflower-This low-carb veggie is eaten alone in fresh or frozen packets, tossed into olive oil and fried, mashed into flaky potatoes, shredded and used as a rice place in main dishes, crusted with low-carbon and keto pizzas, and many more

8. Frozen chicken tenders – Have a big bag on hand; easily thaw and barbecue, saute, combine with veggies and top with low-carbohydrate garlic sauce, use in chicken alfedo, chicken piccata, tacos, indigenous butter chicken, and more.

9. Ground beef – Make a broad burger and top with all kinds of food, from cheese, sauteed mushrooms, grilled onions ... or crumble and cook taco or taco shells; add in lettuce, avocado, and cheese, sour taco cream for a tortilla taco salad.

10. Almonds (flavored or plain)-these are delicious and nutritious snacks; but, please hold them while you eat while they add up the carbs. Habanero, cocoon, salt and vinegar, and more are the flavors.

The keto diet is the flexible and fascinating way to lose weight with many tasty options for food. fridge, freezer, and larder, and you'll be able to add some tasty delicacies and snacks in the morning.

Anyone who wants to lose weight can get a ketogenic diet healthier choice. Visit Balanced Keto, a helpful resource that helps dietors to access food ideas and dietary information.

Net Carbs

Net carbs are carbohydrates which the body can digest and process as dietary carbohydrate. Therefore, blood sugar is directly affected. You will calculate how many net carbs you consume by taking the nutrition, glycerin, and sugar alcohol grams out of the total carbohydrate. Net carbs are the only carbs you have to rely on for low-carb diets, such as the Atkins diet.

It is important to see why fibers are not normal carbohydrates. The fiber material does not break down into sugar, so it does not take part in the carbohydrate's total sugar load. When a bread slice has 27 grams of carbohydrate and a total of 3 grams of fiber, it is simply 24 grams carbohydrate (27 g – 3 grams = 24 grams). This explains why certain high-fibre foods can influence blood sugar and insulin levels more favorably.

Only herbal foods provide dietary fiber. Fiber has a variety of benefits and some more negative effects on digestion. One beneficial impact is that fiber can decelerate food digestion. This results in the food being progressively drained into the small intestine from the stomach. This ensures that large amounts of glucose can be easily absorbed from the small intestine into the blood and are less likely to result from an insulin outbreak. Insulin is the hormone released from the small gut as glucose is ingested. It is likely that slowing down the emptying of the stomach helps prevent the body from releasing large amounts of insulin due to frequent fast glucose releases into the intestine. In fact, this will help protect prone people from diabetes.

However, fiber is hampered by the absorption of some nutrients. For example, up to 5% of fat is not absorbed by this intrusion in a moderately high fiber diet. This is also good in Australia, as 63% of men and 47% of women in 1995 were overweight, without any indication of decreasing the rate of overweight and obesity. The absorption of a number of essential minerals or trace elements is often interfered with by the high fiber diet, but a high fiber diet would often provide you with extra minerals and trace elements so that the effect is not considered to be very important for regular western diets.

Despite these mild adverse effects, a high intake of fibers is shown to be substantially beneficial throughout. Among the main causes of constipation is low fiber intake, particularly in insoluble forms of fibers such as in bread and other wheat products. Low fiber consumption is also closely related to an increased risk of diverticulitis. Although less persuasive, the lack of fiber in the diet may also lead to rectal cancer, hemorrhoids, obesity, appendicitis, and colitis ulcers. The high intake from the fruits, vegetables, rolling oats, and saponins found in legumes, insoluble fibres, such as pectin and gum, is related to reduced blood cholesterol. The high intake of herbal foods, which all contain some fiber, is associated with a reduced risk of cardiovascular disease, cancer, and an improved life expectancy.

Another advantage, and one that can help to maintain weight, is the feeling of satiety, a sense of fullness that accompanies a rich meal in fiber.

It is also true that high fiber foods are almost always fat-low so that a high fiber diet is typically a low-fat diet.

Net carbs are another term for carbohydrates stored in the body's systems as dietary carbohydrates. Net carbs affect your blood sugar directly. You derive the grams of fiber, glycerine, and sugar alcohol from the number of grams of carbs you have consumed to help calculate your intake. The net carb remains. This is the amount you use for items like the Atkin diet. You must know that fiber is not a carbohydrate. In your system, fiber does not turn into sugar, so it does not work like a sugar load in your body. For example, if a loaf of bread has 27 grams of carb and 3 grams of fiber, you have 24 grams of net carbide. The fiber cancels the fat, gram by gram.

High fiber foods can affect your blood sugar. Plants are the only dietary fiber available. Many fiber advantages impact the digestive tract. It slows your food absorption, which ensures you get more nutrients in your food and prevent blood sugar spikes or insulin surges. Insulin is a hormone that your small intestines release when glucose is absorbed. Fiber helps to prevent you from producing too much insulin by stopping the digestion. This will help the body consume the right nutrients better and keep many people from developing diabetes.

For example, approximately 5% of the fat you eat can be flushed with a high diet of fibre. A typical Westerner's regular diet will not be adversely impacted by the few minerals blocked by fiber since the slow digestion will consume several more minerals and vitamins. A high-fiber diet is mostly much more advantageous. The low fiber intake in many diets is also a big cause of constipation, which can cause too much trouble. It also causes rectal and hemorrhoid cancer, appendicitis, ulcerative colitis, and diverticulitis.

Low-Carb and Keto Diet Fast Food Menu Choices: How to Eat Successfully at Restaurants

For those that eat low carb or keto diets, in any fast food or restaurant, there's almost always plenty to eat. Plan ahead. Plan ahead. Check their menu and nutrition details online at home or by using your mobile before joining a restaurant. It is always essential to know the healthy options before you are tempted by carbohydrate food.

I have compiled a list of several restaurants and fast-food locations, which I find to be the lowest (and most emotionally satisfying) choice, to facilitate finding a quick-keto-friendly alternative. They are not all ideal options, but if you don't have any choice because of the time or venue constraints, you do it in a pinch.

Quick food places are a major aid in postponing the nutritious content. Every day it becomes easier to obey the keto diet. The number of carbs that I mention is estimated and NET grams.

Usually, there is some salad option wherever you are. Remove the bun at Burger joints, and several places sell salad wraps. Chicken needs not to have breading. Breading.

It helps, as a side note, to have a handy knife in your car or wallet. In tiny pieces of salad, tall, juicy burgers end up at the table or in the lap. Tiny, flimsy fast-food plasticware is also hard to eat. Remove and enjoy your own robust utensils!

Now for choices of food ... Here are some usually very obvious guidelines to follow:

- Skip the wrap or bun
- Skip potato, rice, or pasta
- Salads- no croutons. Ranch, blue cheese, Caesar, chipotle-low sugar dressing options. See the name that gives you an indication, something like "honey" in the sweet dressing or "sweet" in the name; these are not typically a good choice. Check the ingredient for products with higher carbohydrates.
- Chicken – Pick either grilled or sprinkled. Keep away from any breaded chicken.

McDonald's-go for any burger grilled chicken (2 g) or (zero-g) that has no bun and is filled with mayo, mustard, oignons, and so on. No ketchup. No ketchup. Attach side lettuce (3 g). Caesar's salad of grilled chicken or the grilled chicken bacon salad is 9 g.

Burger King: Burger (null g) without the topped and bun with mayo, cheese, onions, mustard ... The same burger information is given by McDonald's. No ketchup. No ketchup. Without the bun, the tender grill chicken sandwich is 3 g. BEWARE – you will think the veggie burger is tiny, but 19 g of carbs, so the whole day of the keto carbs is around. BEWARE. Attach side lettuce (3 g). The garden salad with tender grill is 8 g without dressing or croutons. The chicken salad is not an option. Do not try. Do not try.

BONUS- -- freshly fried apple and 5 g of net carbs with caramel sauce are not fried.

Subway-Subway can probably miss if you can. The buns and wraps are rich in carbohydrates. I suppose you might just have them put in a wrapper sans bun with the ingredients, but that doesn't sound enticing. I have no details about how many carbs any single bunless subs would have been, but you probably can find it out-chicken or pepperoni is good, but "sweet onion" chicken is all right? No idea. No idea. Stick to the salads, but just get iceberg lettuce (4 g).

Carl's Junior and Hardees-This chain offers a "lettuce wrap" wrapped in a large piece of lettuce for quick low-carb consumption. I like to wear my own fork in place.) Six-dollar burger (7 g), 1/2 thick-burger (5 g), charcoal chicken club sandwich (7g/10 g in Hardees) Bunless Options. Without croutons, grilled chicken salad is 10 g. The salad on the side is 3 g.

The unwich, Jimmy John's sandwich wrapped in salad-works in this bill. Food is okay, just make sure the ingredients are not high in emissions.

Wendy's – Again, in a lettuce wrap or a package, you can bring your burger. Any topping burger. Mayo's got maize syrup and is 1 g. The fillet of the chicken grill is 1 g. You can order it in the chicken sandwich or the supreme sandwich of the chicken grill. Best salads: chicken caesar (7 g), grilled chicken salad. Side salads for Caesar 6 g or 2 g.

Pizza hut and other pizza locations-Pizza without crust can be consumed. You have to eat twice, but if you can't stop a party or dinner at the pizza, just slip off a cheesy top and eat the huge messy pile of cheese and toppings. A side salad is a good extra. Otherwise, I just prefer to make pizza with low-carbon crusts at home.

Mongolian Grill-YES! Load the bowl with chicken, shrimp, onion, and mushrooms and then add the black bean sauce of Asia. I know that beans have carbohydrates, but this label says 1 gram of carbohydrates per unit (every sauce is a label). Put a little bit of garlic and wait before the griller does his job. You obviously miss the appetizers, tortillas, and rice. Ask the waiting workers not to carry them to the table.

Italian restaurants – they take a little smartness, but they can be frustrating! Ideas: how about the Italian chicken Marsala? Make sure the pasta doesn't come in. Replace broccoli or some other keto-friendly side dish-or a large salad. Chicken piccata is also a chance.

Mexican and Chinese restaurants are the toughest as any low carb alternative is not, first and foremost, the reason for going to the restaurant. I like to get a big burrito without boobs at a Mexican restaurant and spread the soft tortilla like a platform. Eat the ingredients inside and throw the tortilla.

You can find choices if you MUST go to the Chinese buffet (I have attended a funeral dinner one day), but they probably won't be your favorite General Tso. What about the options of the salad bar? Eggs? Eggs? Eggrolls insides, and I also ate just the insides of the crab rangoons. Sadly, those ideas leave on your plate a lot of discarded shells and deep-fried outer parts and look like a real waste of food.

Wings anywhere-Basic buffalo sauce is usually okay as well as Parmesan garlic.

Comfort shops can also be a good choice! 7-11 has boxes of hard-boiled eggs, slabs of cheese, slim jims, almonds, and rinds of pork. The pork rinds come with the taste of barbecue and are ZERO carbs.

Remember, keep the potatoes, bread, noodles, rice, fries, and tortillas in your mind, whatever you want. And watch for maize starch, bread crumbs, and other fillers. With careful preparation and good behavior, balanced eating choices and low carbon alternatives are available, and an effective eating plan can be adhered to.

The ketogenic diet is a good way to lose weight for everyone. Visit Safe Keto, a helpful resource where dietarians can access food ideas and dietary knowledge.

CHAPTER THREE: KETOGENIC DIET PLAN

Keto diets have really come on hard. It is a perfect way not only to easily dump off these extra pounds but also to remain well and safe. It's more than just a diet for those who have tried and are now on the Keto Diet. It's a way of life, a whole new way of life. But it is not easy, as any big change in life, but it needs unbelievable dedication and determination.

Nice for others, but not for everyone? -- While a ketogenic diet was used to dramatically increase the quality of life, certain people do not share the ways of thinking of the majority. But why exactly is that? As we can recall, the only way we can get rid of the excess weight was to avoid eating unhealthy foods, which we are used to eating every day. So if you instruct people to consume healthy fats (The main word is healthy), you can definitely understand why people are doubtful how and why they consume more fat to lose weight and do it quickly. This idea goes against all the weight loss we ever knew.

There really is nothing to fear if you're open to a little technology when it comes to changing your diet. Changing your diet can be very frustrating for many people. Particularly if they feel uncontrolled, especially when they are told they have to follow a particular treatment to better treat a chronic condition or dislike discomfort in the normal way.

The ketogenic diet is a popular program for weight loss. It uses high-fat and very low carbohydrates to burn fat rather than glucose. Many people know the Atkins diet, but the keto plan eliminates carbohydrates even more. Since we are surrounded by fast foods and processed foods, avoiding high-carb foods can be a challenge, but careful preparation can help. Here are a couple of products of a keto diet.

Tips for You to Start

1. If you cook just for yourself, freeze or cool the remainder of the portions or half the recipes if appropriate.

2. Feel free to trade lunch for dinner, lunch for breakfast, etc ... on the same day. If you like, you can even switch the entire days.

3. Make the **keto buns** in advance (the complete recipe of 10 can be made). Freeze the night before or in the oven just before serving, to hold fresh and defrost at room temperature.

4. No snacks should be required between meals, but make sure that you get some keto-friendly snacks. Here is a list of snacks that you can try, and a full diet list is given here to complete **Keto Diet List**.

5. Very low-carb diets (less than 30 grams of net carbohydrates) are sometimes magnesium deficient. I recommend that you take magnesium supplements or add magnesium-high snacks like nuts. Also, if you have any keto-flu symptoms, make sure to eat extra sodium (I use rosé Himalayan salt)

6. You do not have to make minor changes to this diet plan for everyone. Reduce portions of meat and eggs if you need less protein. Don't worry about little **excess protein**; it won't kick you out. Protein simply keeps hungry. When adding more fat (or less), concentrate on adding oils and fatty foods when making the changes. Using KetoDiet Buddy to find your perfect macros!

7. Some recipes in total carbs and fiber are higher. If you fear that fiber will harm your weight loss,: Total Carbs or Net Carbs: What does it really matter? Possibly, fiber will help you lose weight.

8. If you're not hungry, don't feed, even if it means that you're going to save your food.

CONCLUSION

Good dieting for weight loss is a diet that does not in any way impact your overall health. The reality is that there are people who prefer fad diets that end up compromising their health. For example, while it is advisable to minimize your consumption of carbohydrates in order to lose weight, it is not advisable at all to cut the food group entirely out of your diet. You actually have to pick healthy carbs and take them in the right proportions so that you can match calories in and calories out.

Keto and low-carb dietitians realize they need to prepare ahead before they visit fast-food restaurants. It's nice to be armed with some healthier choices before being tempted by the menu items that you're not supposed to have on a low-carb diet. If you are to make it easy to find a quick keto-friendly alternative, we have compiled a list of several restaurants and fast food venues and items that we have found to be the lowest (and most emotionally satisfying) choice. These aren't always the best options, but when you're left with no other options due to time or place constraints, they're going to do it in a pinch.

In order to understand why the Keto Diet is bad in the long run, you need to understand how the Ketogenic Diet functions. A Keto Diet is one that is very low in carbohydrates, which is one of the key sources of nutrition for the body.

www.ingramcontent.com/pod-product-compliance
Ingram Content Group UK Ltd.
Pitfield, Milton Keynes, MK11 3LW, UK
UKHW022218230426
12048UKWH00016BA/920